8 Day Devotional

Start Healing From the Sting of Rejection

You can move from that place of pain once you understand the levels of healing.

Joy Roberson

Copyright © 2024 by Joy Roberson

No part of this book may be reproduced or transmitted in any form or by any means, graphic, mechanical, including photocopying, recording, taping or by permission in writing from the author or publisher.

Unless otherwise indicated, all scripture quotations are from the KJV or NIV of the bible.

About the author, Joy Roberson

I am a woman of integrity,I live my life accordingly by precept and example. I trust God's power and guidance. I respect His authority. I am a manifested miracle. I walk in God's authority and strength. My smile is contagious; it reflects my inner self. I have endured many challenges and overcome them all,I had many falls and times I felt I wouldn't find my way back up but I did everything I endured. I have four gifted children, three grandchildren, and four siblings that mean the world to me. I have many more sons and daughters that adopted me to be their mother. Professionally, I am a hairstylist. I studied Master education in 2017 to become a cosmetology instructor. I love God, I love life,and I love laughter. I encourage everyone to live accordingly.Dream big, make your dreams manifest, Let what's in you come out no matter who doesn't believe in your vision,prove it!

Prevention

Suicide prevention lifeline: 1-800-273-8255

Alcohol Anonymous: 1-800-232-463

AIDS and HIV 1-800-232-4636

Child Abuse: 1-800-422-4453; Crisis Text Line: Text home to 741741

gambler anonymous188-628-9454

Narcotic Anonymous domestic violence hotline: 1-800-799-7233

To contact the Veterans Crisis Line, text 988, then press the number 838-255.

Substance Abuse and Mental Health 1-800-662-4357

sexual assault 1-800-656-4673

Dedication

To my late parents I am grateful of , Johnnie Lee Roberson and Lavenia Jackson (Mattie Brown), as well as my husband, Gregory Lee, who was my high school sweetheart. My children Shebrelle Brown, Kenneth Brown Jr., J'Lohn Marks, and Caleb Marks. I cherish my three grandchildren and my four siblings. R.I.P. to one of them Lisa Roberson.

8 Day Devotional

Start Healing From the Sting of Rejection

From the Desk of Joy Roberson

Greetings to you in Jesus name. The Holy Spirit guided the writing and inspiration of this book. As you read this book, The words will pierce your heart and fill the voids in your soul this book shift your mindset and bring healing to your circumstances. You must possess the will and mentality to permit the restoration of your life and the healing of your spirit from the traumas of rejection in your past. Don't expect those who hurt you to apologize,often they won't. God promises to heal you, let Him.

God Bless!!!

Joy Roberson Lee

Preface

If you've experienced a living hell and believe that death is preferable to life, or if you believe that others things will alleviate your pain. If you are ready to walk into all God has for you, you are reading the right life plan book. Let me pose a few questions to you, and if you answer any of them negatively, it's a clear indication that the Lord has called you to purchase this book.

1. Do you know your purpose in life? Who are you?

2. Are your past hurts still tormenting you? Be honest.
3. Do you know that some blessings come after you have endured hardship in God's timing?
4. Do you know that the price is worth all you've gone through?
5. Do you know God has already felt your pain?
6. Have you taken any steps towards healing through professional counseling or spiritual advisors?

7. Do you know that the best way to discover who you are is to know God and His redemption or salvation after you receive Jesus as your savior?

Your past will never stop its the devil job to manipulate you; this is his task. He knows how to proceed with you, as the Lord has counted his days in your life. I'm trying to remind you that this is a demonic distraction that is meant to cause delays. You have to stay focused and be strong. You must exert all your energy to combat the enemy and his tactics. He poses a serious threat and seeks to impede your progress. Some of us bear visible scars, while others bear invisible scars. The invisible scars are those that are either dead or deeply cut, and may have been caused by rejection. Rejection is painful, but you must understand that God, or others don't always say yes this type of rejection sets you up for a bigger yes in your latter season, and all things will be good. Romans 8:28 states, "We know that all things work for good for those who love God, who are called according to his purpose." A rejected soul is accompanied by several spirits which are critical to your mind and soul to name a few fear, intimidation, offense, and insecurities. These things carry negative energy and will be very detrimental to your relationships with others. Rejection often keeps you in a dark place of isolation, and isolation is not good because you become your own worst enemy. Come out of that dark, empty place. As time goes on, it's not even the rejection that hurts you anymore; it's the thoughts and reminders. It's not always the fall that's harmful, but the act of falling and failing to get up. Get up from that place. Rejection is part of God's plan for your life to grow you up. Yes, to mature and push you into a lifestyle of fasting and prayer. Many blessings from God are undeserved; we must pay for them along our life journey through hardship, trial and error. Some of us don't want to endure the work that comes with the things we ask God to do; they want to skip the process as soon as they feel a little pain and go straight to the blessing. Sometimes pain comes with territory. God brings out the best in us during certain seasons; he is merely preparing you for your true identity—he withholds certain things from us until he is confident in your ability to handle them. Healing is vital. You can't really trust a hurt person. You don't know your strength until you've persevered through the process. The worst part is over at that pointthen comes your joy, peace, and strength. What does it take to establish you? 1 Peter 5:10 says, "And after you have suffered a little while, the God of all grace, who called you to His eternal glory in

Christ, will himself restore, confirm, strengthen, and establish you."

Day 1: Repent

No matter what we do in life, we should always strive to maintain a healthy line of communication with God. The first and most important step is to repent of our sins. In certain instances,you may perform the act of sinning without knowing it remember sin separate you from God; how do you repent?" As stated in Matthew chapters 3 and 2, repent, for the kingdom of God is near. What it means to repent is to transform your inner self from the way you always think, and to live your life in a way that demonstrates that you have repented. Ensure your inner self aligns with the external portrayal. There are some people who have a form and style of godliness, but they deny the power that comes with it. Do not mislead others; your life and thoughts should align with God's word and His desire for you. If you are a leader, you must live by example, because people are watching you. When you lead a life of repentance, your actions should not mirror your old habits. You are the problem if you think you can think the same way; you must show change. This is why Jesus died. If your old way of living and thinking is not good, then Jesus died for you. To be born again, you must be redeemed from your old man. Someone is depending on you. Don't allow the adversary to use the things you've done to enslave you John 8:32b (NIV)says

"Then you will know the truth, and the truth will make you free."

A gathering of believing Jews is the audience to whom Jesus is preaching. He elaborates in the lines that follow (John 8:31–36) that His true disciples are those who follow His instructions without deviation. In contrast to being spiritually enslaved to sin, he is spiritually free. If you follow Jesus, you will live forever (John 14:6). When He declares, "I am the way, the truth, and the life," He is referring to Himself and His teachings as the truth. To have a true knowledge of Jesus and what He gives requires more than just a theoretical comprehension; it necessitates direct experience and meaningful relationships. In this context, truth stands for God's revelation, which includes knowing God's character, purpose, and will via Jesus. As so, it is an indication of the truth of redemption, the gospel, and the end of sin. "The truth will set you free" refers to a liberation from the shackles of sin, which is a spiritual liberation. Sin enslaves people before they know Christ (John 8:34), but when they learn and believe the truth about Jesus, they are set free from sin's power and judgment. A release from the shackles of sin by faith in Christ leads to a life illuminated by God's grace, truth, and everlasting life. It's liberation from sin's consequence, terror, and guilt. Knowing and accepting Christ's truth leads to spiritual freedom, as taught in John 8:32b. It's an exhortation to follow Jesus as a disciple, and staying rooted in his teachings is the way to eternal freedom from sin, death, and God's separation.

You are free now. Every day, live and stay in God's word. In verses 23–24 of Psalm 37, we read of God's care and direction for people who put their trust in Him. He supports and maintains them even when they falter. In verse 25, we read that God is faithful in providing for the needs of the righteous. The righteous can rely on God no matter what happens to them because He does not leave them. Blessings and Generosity (v. 26): The righteous, who have faith in God's providence, are blessed because they are living a righteous life (v. 27): The psalm urges readers to reject wickedness and seek instead the good things that will bring them safety and everlasting life.

Relationship Between the Two Chapters:

Psalm 37:23–27 and John 8:32b both speak about being free and secure in God. Following God's virtuous path results in direction, provision, and blessing (Psalm 37:23–27), whereas understanding the truth (Jesus) offers spiritual liberty (John 8:32b). Having faith in God's care and doing what He wants are both encouraged in these verses. When one puts their trust in Jesus Christ, they are set free from sin, guilt, and death anxiety, and this leads to spiritual freedom. Living in accordance with God's truth, purpose, and identity enables one to experience life to the fullest, just as God intended. Having one's life changed by relationship with God is what it means to be spiritually free.

Day 2: Forgive Others

The Bible provides several compelling reasons why we should forgive others. Forgiveness is central to Christian teaching, rooted in God's character and His forgiveness toward humanity. If you are a born-again Christian, this should be effortless for you. To forgive someone means to stop harboring resentment or anger toward them for any wrongdoing. For some people, this is a difficult concept to grasp. Individuals who have wronged you, shown unkindness, or inflicted pain on you demonstrate genuine forgiveness. Sometimes the situation may not be as bad as it seems, but it's up to you to forgive yourself and move on from the past. With the right attitude, moving on and forgiving does not mean you will not suffer or forget your freedom. Matthew 6:14–15 says, "For if you forgive others their trespasses, your heavenly Father will also forgive you; but if you do not forgive others, neither will your Father forgive your trespasses." The refusal to forgive one's own transgressions is a condition that God will not pardon, according to some interpretations of the text. People have a difficult time forgiving individuals who have wronged them, which makes processing this information challenging.

It Is Jesus's Direct Instructive

Forgiveness was a clear mandate from Jesus to His disciples. Actually, for Christians, forgiveness is a must.

Bible verse 14–15 (NIV) OF Matthew 6 says,"If you are willing to forgive others when they wrong you, your heavenly Father will do the same. Your Father will not forgive your sins unless you forgive the sins of others."

Just to clarify: According to Jesus, our capacity to have fellowship with God is proportional to the degree to which we are able to forgive others. If we can't forgive other people, we'll never be able to experience God's forgiveness.

The Character of God is Reflected in Forgiveness

God is a forgiving and caring God who expects His children to do the same. "Be merciful, as your Father is merciful" (NIV, Luke 6:36–37). You won't be judged if you don't pass judgment. Keep silent, and no one will speak poorly of you. Giving a little forgiveness goes a long way. We show the mercy and grace of God by forgiving those who have wronged us. When we decide to forgive instead of clinging to resentment or animosity, we provide witness to His mercy.

Holding grudges Brings on Resentment and Damage

The individual carrying the grudge and their relationships with others are both harmed by the bitterness that results from holding onto unforgiveness. Hebrews 12:15 says: "See to it that no one falls short of the grace of God and that no bitter root grows up to cause trouble and defile many. "Refusing to forgive causes us to harbor bitterness, wrath, and resentment. Not only may these bad feelings damage us, but they can also permeate our relationships and lead us astray from the love and peace that God offers.

Healing and Freedom Are Brought About by Forgiveness.

We gain healing and freedom when we forgive, and it's not only for the offender's benefit. It frees us from the weight of bitterness, grief, and wrath. Isaiah 18:21–22 (NIV): "I tell you, not seven times, but seventy-seven times," Jesus says in response to Peter's question about how often he should forgive, suggesting an infinite need for mercy. Emotional and spiritual healing are made possible via forgiveness. It allows us to move on peacefully by lifting the burden of unresolved hurt. We break free from the shackles of the past when we forgive.

Forgiveness Fosters Peace and Reconciliation

In order to mend damaged relationships, forgiveness is essential. For one's own healing and the healing of one's Christian community, it is crucial.

Romans 12:18 says, "If it is possible, as far as it depends on you, live at peace with everyone." Peace can be achieved via forgiveness. As in personal relationships, it aids in mending fences and brings people together, both of which are vital in the Christian community.

Forgiveness Was Modeled by Jesus on the Cross

Even in His last moments, Jesus forgave His crucified enemies. This is one of the most moving displays of forgiveness ever seen.

34 of Luke 23 says, "Jesus said, 'Father, forgive them, for they do not know what they are doing.'" Jesus' selfless deed of pardon on the cross exemplifies His boundless compassion and kindness. He forgave His enemies even though He was deeply wounded. No matter how tough it becomes, His disciples are commanded to follow His example and forgive.

Love is Shown via Forgiveness

An act of forgiveness is a deep manifestation of love. Love, according to the Bible, forgets wrongs. 1 Corinthians 13:4-5 states, "Love is patient, love is kind...it keeps no record of wrongs." Forgiveness is a feature of genuine love. Forgiveness is a beautiful expression of the grace, patience, and unconditional love that God has shown us.

To sum up, the Bible teaches that we should forgive others as God has forgiven us. To forgive is to obey and to love at the same time. The character of God is reflected in it, relationships are healed, and the weight of bitterness and hatred is lifted. It is our duty as Christ's disciples to model the kindness and forgiveness that God extends to us.

Day 3: Forgive Yourself

1 John 1:9 says, "If we confess our sins, he is faithful and just to forgive us our sins and to cleanse us from all unrighteousness.". If we repent and seek God's forgiveness, he will wash us clean of all sin, according to this scripture. Although God is aware of our misdeeds, confessing them shows that we agree with God that they are wrong. If we fail to forgive ourselves, it hinders our love for others. Our love for others facilitates self-forgiveness. 1 Corinthians 13:4-5 in the

Bible states that love is patient and kind and does not envy, boast, or pride itself: Love does not insist on its own way; it is not irritable or resentful; it does not rejoice at wrong, but rejoices in the right." It's challenging to love others, right? If you don't love yourself, those who hurt others will continue to hurt others as long as they do. You've got to move from that place of pain and rejection. You will be critical to those who love you as long as you are a prisoner to yourself. Your mind, body, and soul are captive. You cannot help others if you can't help yourself spiritually. You are powerless, and your witness is ineffective with others until you see yourself free. **BE FREE!!!**

Isaiah 43:25 says, "I, am he who blots out your transgressions, for my own sake, and remembers your sins no more." This verse serves as covenantal language, assuring God's people of the forgiveness of their sins.

In order to stress how comprehensive God's forgiveness is, the passage makes use of visual descriptions:

"Blotting out" is the process of erasing written text. God has wiped the pages of Israel's transgressions clean, like a book. In the future, God will not remember Israel's transgressions and punish them.

"I, even I, am he": This saying highlights who God is and how powerful he is. By emphasizing "I," God emphasizes that no one else can forgive and erase sin from the universe. It emphasizes once again that repentance and forgiveness are gifts from God and not human efforts.

Repetition of God's Sovereignty emphasizes

that no one else can make. A one-of-a-kind holy deed is set in motion.

2. "Blots out your transgressions": The term "blots out" means to completely remove sin from your life. Paper could be easily cleaned or wiped clean in ancient times since ink did not leave a permanent stain. In a symbolic sense, God is erasing the record of the people's transgressions, as if they had never occurred. Intentional disobedience and defiance of God is transgressions. God deals with willful sin when he forgives trespasses, not only accidental or careless acts. The

term "blotting out" describes God's action of completely removing sin from history, rather than merely ignoring it. As if the transgressions had never occurred, the act of "blotting out" suggests total pardon. Thirdly, the phrase "for my own sake" is highly crucial. People don't merit God's forgiveness; rather, it is a result of His character and intentions. He chooses to forgive because He is loving and merciful, and because He has a covenant relationship with His people. For the Glory of God: God's mercy and grace are shown via His forgiveness. For the purpose of His own honor, righteousness, and fulfillment of His promises, His acts. He maintains His character as a caring and compassionate God by pardoning sins. The promise that God would be their God in the covenant that He made with the Israelites is echoed here. The basis for this forgiveness is His unwavering commitment to His own nature and promises.

"Remember your sins no more": This statement indicates that God has decided not to remember or punish them for their transgressions anymore. God knows everything, so it's not that He can't remember; it's that He chooses not to remember their transgressions when dealing with them. It means you're completely and totally forgiven. God's "forgetting" is an intentional display of grace. He chooses to move on from their mistakes and forgives them. What this means is that what happened in the past does not matter to God or His people anymore; what matters is that they are no longer relevant. The fullness of God's forgiveness is demonstrated in this remark, which pertains to the restoration of relationships. He restores fellowship with His people by erasing their shame and letting them go of their transgressions. In order to forgive sins, God must take the initiative. God chooses to forgive the people's sins because He loves them and because they didn't deserve it. Grace, which is a favor from God that is not due, is reflected here. Expressed so forcefully in this text is the grace of God. It is not human decency but God's character that justifies forgiveness. He shows His mercy and unfaltering love by forgiving for no other reason than to do so.

Reestablishing fellowship between the sinner and God is the essence of God's forgiveness. By erasing his transgressions from memory, he effectively removes them as a defining factor in their future relationship. A new beginning and revitalization are present.

The condition for God's forgiveness is that He will fulfill His covenant obligations. His character dictates that He will always be faithful to His people, including Israel. In spite of our frailty, He never strays from His word.

When God decides to forgive, it is a full and unconditional forgiveness (Isaiah 43:25). That God is merciful and forgets our transgressions after He has forgiven them is a comforting thought. Knowing that God's forgiveness is provided out of love for His own reason and not because we deserve it, this verse encourages us to put our trust in God's grace.

In light of God's grace, it exhorts us to be

humble, thankful, and committed to continuing to walk in faith and obedience so that we may keep the relationship we have been restored.

Day 4: Praying for Direction

Proverbs 16:9 states that although we make our own plans, the Lord still directs us, arranging our lives and organizing our paths to achieve our goals. At times, God intervenes without our consent, interrupting our plans to protect us from the unseen. This is known as his permissive will. This typically occurs when we have desires or cravings that are outside God's will, directing our paths accordingly.

Proverbs 20:24 states, "A man's steps are from the Lord; how then can man understand his way?" This proverb conveys that God is in control of everything, and that people will not always understand the circumstances they face. Proverbs teaches us 2 things:

Have Faith: Have faith in God, for He will lead you in the right path. It is naive to think that humans can comprehend everything on par with God.

God never leads anyone wrong. God also forbids anyone from succumbing to overwhelming temptations.

Relying on one's own discretion: When people rely too heavily on their own discretion, they can make poor decisions.

Psalm 37:23-24 says, "The LORD establishes a man's steps when he delights in his way. The LORD upholds his hand, preventing him from falling."

According to some, these verses are reassuring and motivating. Other possible interpretations include:

- God watches over you.
- Conceal God's word deep within your soul.
- He gives you strength to get up after falling.

James 4:3 says, "You ask and do not receive, because you ask wrongly to spend it on your passions." The interpretation of this verse suggests that Christians were attempting to control God by requesting items to fulfill their personal desires, rather than pursuing their genuine desires. James continues by comparing following the knowledge of this world to adultery, or "cheating" on God. He exhorts Christians to turn away from sin, accept God's grace, be humble, and break ties with the world. Psalm 78:18 says, "They tempted God in their heart by asking meat for their lust" in the King James Version.

In the following verses, the people speak against God, saying, "Can God furnish a table in the wilderness?" God responds by smiting the rock, causing waters to gush out and streams to overflow. Hebrews 11:6 says, " And without faith, it is impossible to please God, because anyone who comes to him must believe that he exists and that he rewards those who earnestly seek him."You are an overcomer! You are free to let God lead your pathway to enormous and mighty things. Defeat is nothing for you! You have the freedom to follow God's leading as He guides you towards great and powerful things. **Important things to remember:**

1. Even when you can't see the forest for the trees, have faith that God has a plan for your life.

2. Put your trust in Him and He will show you the way to success.

3. In your prayers, seek God's guidance and direction. When you pray earnestly, He will grant you the wisdom you require.

4. Waiting could be difficult, but trust that God's timing is perfect every time. Keep your courage and wait for Him to show you.

5. His intentions when the time is appropriate.

6. If you take the time to read God's Word, He will lead you. The Bible provides us with the knowledge and guidance we need to make choices that are in harmony with God's will.

7. Finding contentment is a gift from God when your decisions are in harmony with His will. Keep praying and asking God for clarification if you're feeling nervous or uncomfortable.

8. Opportunities that God opens or closes

can be a sign of His will. Listen for the opportunities He is presenting to you and put your faith in His leading.

9. It can be helpful to talk to reliable people who are also religious, such as mentors or close friends. Occasionally, God speaks to us through others around us who are wise and knowledgeable.

10. Have faith that God has a plan for your life, even if you don't understand it right now. He will lead you by the hand and His plans are always beneficial.

The Lord is eager to show you the way and

direct your steps. Believe in Him, cry out to Him in prayer, and study His Word, and He will lead you in the right direction. Keep quiet and listen for the serenity He will bring you as you wait for His timing. God is reliable, and He will never abandon you when you need guidance.

Day 5: Get Focused

Focusing clearly involves adapting to the current level of light and developing the ability to perceive clearly whatever captures your attention. If your focus isn't on positive aspects, it's crucial to reroute it towards things that foster growth and positive energy in your mindset. Concentrate on truthful and positive aspects, as the devil will feed you with his falsehoods. Keep in mind, the devil's purpose is to steal, kill, and destroy, but Jesus came to give us abundant life.

Negative energy can lead to numerous distractions, causing you to lose sight of your direction. Take a moment to pray to God about your distractions, and don't be anxious. Philippians 4:6-8 states, "Do not be anxious about anything, but in every situation, present your requests to God through prayer and petition, with thanksgiving." And God's peace, which transcends all understanding, will guard your hearts and minds in Christ Jesus. Finally, brothers and sisters, think about such things: whatever is true, whatever is noble, whatever is right, whatever is pure, whatever is lovely, whatever is admirable—if anything is excellent or praiseworthy." Instead of fretting, Paul says Christians should pray about their problems with an attitude of gratitude. While they do this, they can rest assured that God's peace will surround them. In order to develop a sound and tranquil outlook, he tells students to center their thoughts on virtues like honesty, integrity, loftiness, virtue, purity, and all that is commendable and worthy of praise. Proverbs 19:1 tells us

"Better the poor whose walk is blameless than a fool whose lips are perverse." This proverb emphasizes the value of honesty over money. Even if they are poor, a decent person will be better off than a naive person who talks trash or lies. God values integrity and righteousness more than material prosperity. When we talk about God's will, we're talking about His ideal and all-powerful scheme for people and the world. It includes both His general plans for the universe and His detailed wishes for each person. In order to comprehend God's will, we must acknowledge His omni love, and power and strive to conform our lives to His purposes. Among God's will are His moral precepts for daily life, His sovereign purpose for the universe, and His specific instructions for each person. To do His will, one must have faith, pray constantly, and give one's heart to His plan. The only way to know and do God's will for our lives is to seek Him in all things, including His Word, prayer, and sound advice.

Day 6: Write the Vision

You've got to see your vision before it manifests. Your faith is what moves God and brings all things to manifestation. Habakkuk 2:2 says the Lord will show you in advance.

Psalm 37:23-24 says, "The Lord makes firm the steps of the one who delights in him; though he may stumble, he will not fall, for the Lord upholds him with his hand. These verses make it clear that God leads those who place their trust in Him in the right direction. God will sustain and defend them so that they do not entirely fail, even if they encounter challenges or blunders ("stumble"). God's guiding and sustaining influence keeps believers secure even in trying circumstances. Visions are supernatural visions that appear in dreams, trances, and religious ecstasies. Visions convey revelation and provide more clarity than dreams. Don't share your visions or dreams with others; not everyone will understand things God makes relevant to you. Write them down on paper, just as

God's words tell us what to do. Keep it. This is your secret to God, which you should keep in a safe place until he manifests as a testimony, allowing others to believe what you wrote from your vision. Some people use vision boards for this purpose, but the choice is entirely yours. Without vision, people perish. You're simply existing with a life plan. Don't allow yourself to drift through life without meaning or a plan.

James 1:8 states, "Such a person is double-minded and unstable in all they do."

The individual described in this verse is one who is unable to place their complete trust in God because their ideas or faith are conflicted. Being "double-minded" means that a person lacks stability and consistency, which makes it difficult for them to make judgments that are in their best interests or to carry out their actions appropriately. They are prone to wavering, resulting in instability in every aspect of life. A crucial component of religion is trusting God, which can be tough, particularly in trying times. In order to strengthen your faith in **God, consider the following:**

1. **Realize who God is.**

Gaining a grasp of God's identity fosters trust. God is always good, loving, faithful, and understanding of all things. Lord, you have never abandoned those who seek you; therefore, those who know your name trust you (Psalm 9:10).

Step up: Get to know God better by reading His Word, the Bible. Learn about His character, especially His love and loyalty to

His people. If you are familiar with God's promises and deeds, you will have faith in His reliability.

2. Pray and Seek Assistance

Relationships build trust, and prayer is the means by which we address God. Prayer allows you to express your worries and seek direction. In all circumstances, "do not be anxious, but present your requests to God through prayer and petition, with thanksgiving" (Philippians 4:6-7).

The next step is to pray to God about all of your concerns. In prayer, ask Him to increase your faith and calm you when you feel overwhelmed by fear

3. **Keep in mind God's dependability in the past.**

Think about how God has faithfully served you and Scripture. Because of this, you can believe that He will remain faithful even after this world ends.

I will remember the works of the Lord; yes, I will remember your wonders from ancient times (Psalm 77:11).

Take action by recording in a journal the moments when you felt God's presence or witnessed His handiwork. If you need a reminder of His faithfulness when you're doubting, think of these.

4. Give Up COMMAND

If you want to trust God, you must give Him control of your life and your choices. It is essential to trust that He is always working for the best, even when we cannot see it.

The new international version of Proverbs 3:5-6 reads: "Put your trust in the Lord completely and do not rely on your own wisdom. "Submit all of your endeavors to him, and he will direct your paths." When faced with doubt or difficult choices, intentionally surrender them to God. Say, "I trust You, Lord, and I believe You know what's best for me."

5. Rely on God's Plan

Even though God's timeline differs from ours, it is flawless every time. Having faith entails waiting for His timing and patience. Isaiah 40:31 asserts that those who have faith in the Lord will experience strength. With the grace of eagles, they will soar through the air, never tire or faint. Do something: If you want to be patient, you need to keep in mind that God is working even when it seems like nothing is happening. I hope that his schedule works out for the best in the end.

6. Put Your Hope in God's Promises

Trusting God means having faith that He will carry out the many promises He made in the Bible. "For no matter how many promises God has made, they are 'Yes' in Christ," says 2 Corinthians 1:20. Do something: Think about the promises made in Scripture that are relevant to your life right now. Believe in God and these promises can give you strength and hope.

7. Seek out positive people to surround yourself with.

You can strengthen your faith by surrounding yourself with other Christians who also trust in God. Their prayers, encouragement, and testimonies strengthen your faith. Hebrews 10:24–25 refers to: "And let us think about ways we can encourage one another to love and do good deeds." Whether it's through friendships, Bible studies, or church, surround yourself with people who share your religion. Talk to them about your problems, and ask for their support and prayers. Faith in God is a process that develops during time spent in His presence, in prayer, and in contemplation of His fidelity. It includes giving up control, fixing one's attention on His promises, and waiting patiently for His timing. As your relationship with God grows, you will trust Him more and feel calm when you lean on Him. Trust God with your vision; he will not lead you wrong.

Day 7: Reset

You can't get frustrated or disheartened when you fail to move quickly enough or fast enough in response to God's timing; instead, you must RESET. "To reset" means to set again, or in other words, I just made a fresh or different adjustment. Even though it may feel like you're starting all over, it's a fantastic thing to reset your life because it's a major makeover of your life. Changing up a routine that isn't working for you can be advantageous if you're trying to obtain new results by doing the same things over and over again. IF WHAT YOU ARE DOING IS not giving you a different result, you need to RESET!!!

What to Do to Reset

1. **Realizing you need to reset is the first step. Honestly assess your life and be receptive to alteration.**

In 2 Corinthians 13:5, it says, "Examine yourselves to see whether you are in the faith; test yourselves."

Sometimes you just need to take a deep breath and assess the direction your life is taking. Keep an open heart and mind in case God is asking you to make a change.

2. Seek Grace and Forgiveness from God.

To begin the process of reset, one must embrace God's grace and ask for forgiveness for their mistakes. There is always a fresh start and forgiveness offered by God.

1 John 1:9 points out, "If we confess our sins, he is faithful and just and will forgive

us our sins and purify us from all unrighteousness."

The greatest thing is God's grace, regardless of what has transpired. Just tell Him what you've done wrong, and He will forgive you and start over.

3. Let God Have Control

Trusting in God's direction and will for your life, completely give up control of your plans, anxieties, and problems.

According to Proverbs 3:5-6, "Trust in the Lord with all your heart and lean not on your own understanding; in all your ways submit to him, and he will make your paths straight."

Pray about your life's history, your current situation, and your future plans. Have faith that He will lead you down a better road and that He has a plan.

4. Revitalize Your Mind with the Word of God

If you want to reset your life for good, you have to get your priorities straight according to God's Word. A change occurs as a result of this mental refreshment.

The 2nd verse of Romans 12 says, "Do not conform to the pattern of this world, but be transformed by the renewing of your mind."

Spending time in God's Word can help you think differently. To live in accordance with His will, you must renew your thoughts.

5. Choose a Different Road

Making a firm decision to live in accordance with God's ways, abandoning sinful patterns, and starting over is what we mean when we talk about a life reset.

Ephesians 4:22-24 instructs us, "Put off your old self, which is being corrupted by its deceitful desires...and put on the new self, created to be like God in true righteousness and holiness."

Stop doing things the old way that are holding you back. Make a firm decision to change your path such that it brings glory to God and genuine happiness.

6. Strive for Individual and Group Responsibility

Look for other believers to lean on, who you can encourage and who can keep them responsible.

According to Hebrews 10:24-25, "And let us consider how we may spur one another on toward love and good deeds, not giving up meeting together."

There are people that can help you through this. Put yourself in the company of positive, encouraging people who will cheer you on as you take this next step.

7. Believe in the Transformative Power of God

God has the capacity to make a genuine difference in your life. If you let him, he can make a fresh start for you.

2 Corinthians 5:17 says, "Therefore, if anyone is in Christ, the new creation has come: The old has gone, the new is here!"

You are reborn in Christ. The old has passed away, and the new life that God promises is here for you to live in. If you want the ability to change, trust Him.

No matter your past, God is willing to start over with you. You will be led to a new road as you repent of your sins, fill your head with His Word, and give Him control of your plans. Lean on those who will encourage you and have faith in His ability to change you. Beyond your wildest dreams, God has a magnificent plan and purpose for your life. And he will help you to **RESET!**

Day 8: Don't Look Back

According to the Bible, no one is suitable for God's kingdom if he has put his hand to the plough and then turned back. Just like Lot's wife, who is still in the same place she was when she looked back (Genesis 19:26), you don't want to miss out. Avoid dwelling on the past too much; doing so can cause you to miss out on living in the here and now and setting yourself up for failure in the years to come. If you keep dwelling on the past, you'll never be able to go forward in

God's plans for your life; instead, you'll always be tempted to use the sample pass. Dispatch any uncertainty or second thoughts may Jesus' shed blood wash over your thoughts in the name of Jesus Keep in mind that you are an Overcomer; you have triumphed over rejection and its pain, and God delights in forging new paths for you in the wilderness and creating streams to flow through your desert. Have faith in God and his word; he will bring about his will in due course. According to Isaiah 60:23, he will bring it to pass at the proper moment.

Steps to help you not look back:

Release What Has Been

Keep moving forward; there's no need in wallowing in self-pity over setbacks. God invites us to look forward to the future He has planned for us and gives us a new beginning. "Do not dwell on the past; forget the former things," Isaiah 43:18–19 states. The past isn't something God wants you to dwell on. You are about to experience greater things since he is beginning a new chapter in your life. Release your grip on the past and put your faith in Him for the future.

2. Recovering from Setbacks

Your value is not determined by how others perceive you. You can rest assured that your identity is safe in God's loving care.

Those who are crushed in soul are saved by the Lord, according to Psalm 34:18.

No power, not even death itself, or evil spirits, can "separate us from the love of God that is in Christ Jesus our Lord," as stated in Romans 8:38–39.

I know how painful it is to be rejected, but take comfort in knowing that God is with you. Nothing can ever change His love for you, and He loves you no matter what. Your value is founded in God's estimation of you, not in the opinions of others.

3. Trust in God's Word

Instead of dwelling on the hurt from the past, look to the future that God has promised. There is optimism and direction in his intentions for your life.

With "plans to prosper you and not to harm you, plans to give you hope and a future," the Lord declares in Jeremiah 29:11, "For I know the plans I have for you."

The future that God has for you is really incredible. God has a plan for your life regardless of what you've been through or how many times you've been rejected. Embrace the hope and new beginnings found in His promises.

4. Let Go of Resentment and Forgive

Allow God to heal your suffering and forgive those who have wronged you. Achieving healing and progress requires forgiveness.

In light of how much God forgave you in Christ, "Get rid of all bitterness..." (Ephesians 4:31–32). Forgiveness is not an excuse for wrongdoing, but rather a release from carrying the burden of hurt. Forgiveness and surrendering your pain to God allows Him to mend your wounds and put your peace back into your life.

5. Have Faith in God's Redemption

God is an expert at mending wounded hearts. He has the power to divert rejection toward His greater goal. The locusts will eat your years, and I will repay you, says Joel 2:25. God has the power to turn your trials into opportunities for maturity, insight, and fortitude. If anything seems lost, he can bring it back to life and transform it into something lovely.

6. Proceed with Self-Assurance

Proceed with assurance, for God is on their side and wills wonderful things to happen.

I push on toward the goal to gain the

prize for which God has called me heavenward in Christ Jesus, forgetting what is behind and straining toward what is ahead (Philippians 3:13–14).

No amount of hurt or rejection can compare to God's purpose for your life. You are being carried through this season by God, and He has a big purpose for you. Keep going forward.

Rejection does not make you less valuable, and your history does not make you who you are. God is the source of restoration, healing, and hope for the future. Have faith that He will mend your broken heart, grant you forgiveness for your wrongdoers, and direct your focus to the future. You are cherished, and the most wonderful things are still to come for you.

Acknowledgements

Elanena White, author of numerous works, including "I Am Who God Says I Am," has my deepest gratitude.

The author of Confessions of The Preacher's Daughter is Jennifer Page, I thank her for being an inspiration.

My family and those who have served as inspiration for me.

Dorothy Travis, who encouraged me and served as my coach and motivator.

Dorothy authored "Next Level" and multiple other books.

I thank these strong and courageous women, their strength, and beauty have been an inspiration to me, and for that I am eternally grateful.

Made in the USA
Columbia, SC
17 November 2024